Alphamals
A – Z

Graham Carter

B P P

This A–Z of the animal kingdom
will take you on a voyage of discovery,
from the freezing tundra to the heat
of the savannah. It's a place where
alphabet and animals come together
in perfect harmony.

Meet Graham Carter's *Alphamals*.

A

Armadillo

An armadillo sniffs and snuffles,
digging for ants with big shovel paws.
If danger ever comes his way,
he curls into a tight, hard ball
and keeps safe inside his scaly armor.

B

Bumblebee

A bumblebee flits from flower to flower,
drinking up nectar, gathering pollen.
Back at the nest, she feeds the young,
then flies away to find more food,
buzzing a tune wherever she goes.

C

Crocodile

Lurking in the murky depths,
a crocodile basks in the midday sun.
Her long, strong body is as still as a log,
but she's waiting, watching, set to strike
and snatch her prey in snapping jaws.

D

Dragonfly

With translucent wings and a brightly colored body,
a dragonfly darts in a flash.
She swoops between the river reeds,
searching for her insect prey—
as powerful as she is beautiful.

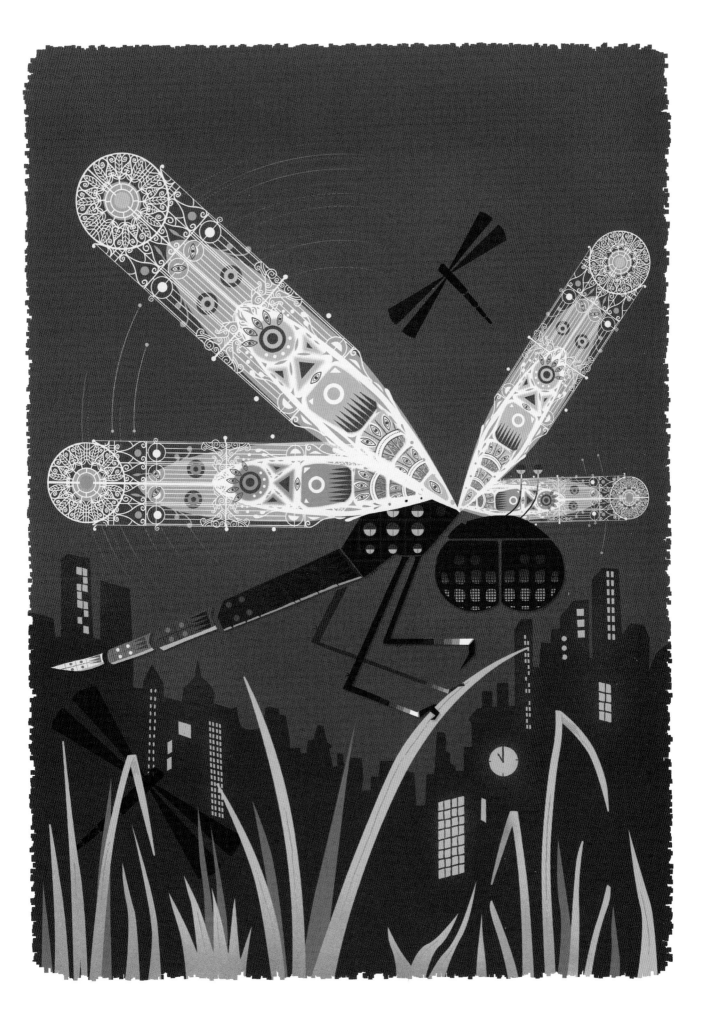

Elephant

An elephant reaches around with her trunk
and scratches her wrinkly back,
then flaps her huge ears to cool herself.
The herd walks many miles a day, trunk to tail,
family and friends all in a line.

Fox

An Arctic fox trots over the snow,
hidden and warm in his ice-white fur.
As the seasons change, his coat does too,
matching the colors of the land —
a predator's cloak of camouflage.

G

Giraffe

A long neck and jet-black tongue
stretch into the treetops, grasping for leaves.
Standing on her long, thin legs,
a giraffe—the tallest animal of all—
towers over the wide savannah.

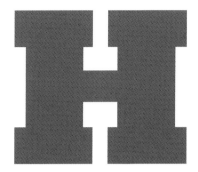

Hedgehog

With a twitching nose and gleaming eyes,
a hedgehog shuffles through the night.
As dawn arrives, he curls up,
a bristling ball of sharp, stiff spines—
a roll of prickles, safe and tight.

I

Iguana

Despite his scales and dragon spikes,
the gentle iguana munches only plants.
This lizard will lounge on rocks or in trees
near rivers and seas, then dive right in,
swimming away with graceful speed.

J

Jaguar

A jaguar lies stretched out, waiting,
high above the forest floor,
her spots concealed among the leaves.
She leaps down quickly, strong and deadly,
catching prey with one sharp bite.

Koala

Up among the eucalyptus branches,
two koalas cuddle in their leafy den,
the baby on its mother's furry back.
Here they'll snooze the day away,
then wake to eat, then snooze some more.

L

Ladybug

A ladybug spreads her black-spotted wings,
then flutters away
on the warm summer breeze.
Her colors warn other creatures
that she is not safe to eat.

M

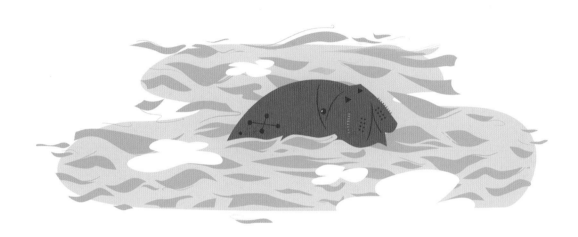

Manatee

Floating in blue lagoon waters,
a manatee drifts with the currents,
a gentle sea cow, chewing grass.
Her paddle tail propels her forward,
steadily, slowly, moving on.

N

Newt

A fire-bellied newt wriggles quickly
through clear, cold pools and icy streams.
His black back is turned to the sky,
but his bright belly flashes a warning sign—
poison, danger, do not eat!

Orangutan

With his thick and shaggy orange hair
and long, strong hands on draping arms,
who could it be but the orangutan?
You'll find him high above the ground,
in the treetops, where he nests and plays.

P

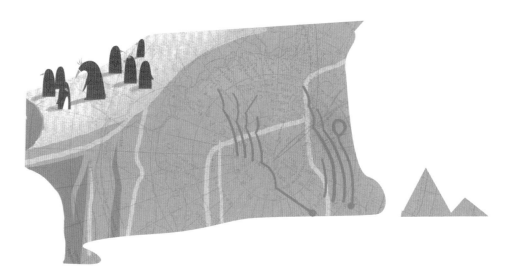

Penguin

With yellow eyebrows and red eyes,
a rockhopper penguin crouches down,
tending his precious eggs.
The wait is long. His mate is fishing now—
preparing for the time the chicks will come.

Quoll

Small but fierce, a little quoll
sleeps through the day, then wakes at night.
With a long, dark snout and speckled coat,
he prowls the shady forest floor,
feasting on birds and other beasts.

R

Rhinoceros

From under the shade of an acacia tree,
a white rhinoceros steps forward,
pawing the ground with one broad foot.
This rare beauty may look slow
but charges with deadly force.

S

Swan

A swan glides up and down the lake.
Parting the mirrored water,
she tilts her head to an elegant angle
and holds up her wings, and just like that there are two—
the swan and her reflection.

Tortoise

A giant tortoise plods along
on leathery legs beneath his high-domed shell.
This ancient creature has seen centuries pass.
Each year, he mates, but otherwise life is slow—
spent eating, sleeping—watching the years go by.

U

Urial

Standing tall above the plain,
a urial displays his mighty horns,
their thick prongs curling out and around.
His shaggy beard hangs long and loose
as his nimble lips pull at the grass.

V

Vulture

With beady eyes and a bald pink head,
a vulture searches for his next meal.
This scavenger will eat anything,
gripping food in his mighty talons
and ripping it up with his sharp, hooked beak.

W

Whale

In freezing polar seas where the white ice floats,
a whale comes up to take a breath.
Then down she dives with a slap of her tail,
deeper and deeper, searching for food,
a giant in the watery depths.

X-ray Tetra

In the dark nighttime waters of the Amazon,
a small bright fish goes gliding by.
His backbone shows through glassy scales
that shimmer in the moonlight,
silver rays dancing on gold-striped fins.

Yak

With shaggy fur and sharp-tipped horns,
a mighty yak stands strong and steady,
unfazed by the wind or the snow.
She moves with her herd, over the hills,
grazing the land whatever the weather.

Zebra

As the sun sets over the wide savannah,
a herd of zebras, zigzag striped,
pause for the night at the river's edge.
A mother nuzzles her newborn foal
while, high above, the stars come out.

To my parents, John and Jackie,
for their amazing support
and encouragement over the years

Text and design copyright © 2017 by The Templar Company Limited
Illustrations copyright © 2017 by Graham Carter

First U.S. edition 2017

Library of Congress Catalog Card Number pending
ISBN 978-0-7636-9557-6

17 18 19 20 21 22 TLF 10 9 8 7 6 5 4 3 2 1

Printed in Dongguan, Guangdong, China

This book was typeset in Rockwell, Coquette, and Mrs Eaves.
The illustrations were created digitally.

BIG PICTURE PRESS
an imprint of
Candlewick Press
99 Dover Street
Somerville, Massachusetts 02144

www.candlewick.com